Big Game Hunting

CHRISTOPHER KAI

FOREWORD BY KEITH FERRAZZI, #1 *NEW YORK TIMES* BESTSELLING AUTHOR OF *NEVER EAT ALONE* AND *WHO'S GOT YOUR BACK*

Praise for *Big Game Hunting*

"I have had the privilege of meeting and working with some of the most inspiring and phenomenal business leaders in the world. Steve Jobs was one of my employees at Atari before he started Apple. Christopher Kai shows you how to meet the 'Steve Jobs' of this generation in his well-written, action-packed book."

—Nolan Bushnell, Founder, Atari and Chuck E. Cheese's, and author of *Finding the Next Steve Jobs: How to Find, Keep and Nurture Creative Talent*

"This book is outstanding. Though we often think of networking as a way to advance our own careers, Christopher looks at how networking can be used for the greater good to help others. I have spent years attending conferences and meeting high-profile leaders and celebrities, yet I was still able to glean so many great tips from this book. I'm giving it to everyone on my team!

—Michelle King Robson, Founder and CEO, EmpowHER, an award-winning social health company for women

"Christopher has been a friend and colleague for many years now. He loves connecting people. He strives to teach and inspire others to become better leaders, so go on this learning journey with him."

—Angy Chin, Former CFO, The Coffee Bean & Tea Leaf

"Christopher uses a powerful and concise analogy to teach you how to effectively network for the most impactful results. The approach he teaches is simple, clear and practical; I don't know anyone in the business world who wouldn't benefit from it."

—Fred Joyal , CEO, Futuredontics, Inc. and co-founder of 1-800-DENTIST

"If you want to bring hope and positive change to the world, you will need a community of friends and influential supporters. Let Chris teach you how to create this community. He has inspired me by being the change we want to see in the world, and I count myself lucky to be his friend. Let his journey inspire you, too."

—Christine Van Loo, World-renowned aerialist and Olympic female Athlete of the Year

"Throughout my decades-long career in the entertainment industry, I have worked with powerhouse celebrities like Michael Jackson, Bruce Springsteen, Quincy Jones, Kenny Rogers, David Foster and Lionel Richie. The key to my success was in how I developed strong relationships with them. My friend Chris has written a fantastic book that shows you how to develop solid relationships so you can have your own powerhouse, successful career."

—Ken Kragen, creator and organizer for "We Are the World," "Hands Across America" and several other historic humanitarian projects.

"I'm the Founder and Executive Director of Omni Nano, a nonprofit that inspires students to learn nanotechnology. Chris' outstanding networking capabilities led to my introduction to a prominent member of my board of directors as well as to Los Angeles' most successful technology entrepreneur, Dr. Patrick Soon-Shiong, a regular on the Forbes 400 wealthiest Americans list. I highly recommend Chris' 'Big Game Hunting' book!"

—Dr. Marco Curreli, Founder and Executive Director, Omni Nano

"Christopher has mastered the art of reciprocity. If you give first, others want to give back to you. Whether you are a startup wanting to raise funds, an entrepreneur who wants to secure bigger clients or a nonprofit seeking donors, this book has priceless advice to help you."

—Tim Chang, Managing Director at Mayfield Fund and one of Forbes Midas List of Tech's Top Investors

Big Game Hunting

Networking with Billionaires, Executives and Celebrities

CHRISTOPHER KAI

KGL

Published in Los Angeles, California, by KGL Publishing, a division of KGL. www.christopherkai.com

ISBN: 978-0-692-45226-4

Cover design by Darin Leach and Thaddeus Vincent Krysiuk

Book design by Vervante

Printed in the United States of America

To anyone who has ever felt
like an outsider.

Contents

Foreword

Growing up in Youngstown, a small steel and coal town outside of Latrobe in southwestern Pennsylvania, I caddied at the local country club in the wealthy town next to mine. I watched, observed and learned from all the successful individuals I met on the golf course. The one thing they all had in common was that they had developed strong and purposeful relationships with other influential individuals. Birds of a feather really did flock together.

Like me, my good friend and colleague Christopher grew up in a small(ish) town: Woodside, Queens, just four miles east of Manhattan, but, in a lot of ways, a world apart. He didn't caddy at the club, but at a young age he learned the importance of developing strong relationships from his Uncle Ding, who ran a small insurance company in lower Manhattan.

Christopher would meet dozens of his uncle's clients, many of whom were successful business owners. Through his uncle and his clients, Christopher got to observe what I saw in the local country club – that if you wanted to be successful in business, you had to befriend what he calls "Big Gamers," individuals in a position of influence.

As the founder and CEO of Ferrazzi Greenlight, a research institute and strategic consulting firm, I have worked with my colleagues to coach hundreds of these corporate influencers on how best to develop stronger relationships with their key leadership teams to reach business objectives. We coach to what I call the four mindsets – generosity, vulnerability, accountability and candor – because they are the foundation to all strong, mutually beneficial relationships.

Christopher has all of these qualities. He's a natural. I've seen him mingle with executives at the Clinton Global Initiative in New York; engage with my employees at Ferrazzi Greenlight, where he has been helping me create a new startup; and connect on a personal level with my 21-year-old son, reaching out and immediately seeking a better understanding of what his interests are and how he could help. Christopher makes his friends feel valued and strangers feel like they are already his friends.

He has done a great service in writing this book. He distills how he has mastered the art of developing solid and impactful relationships and how you can do the same into 20 simple and actionable steps. I hope you find this book as interesting, informative and inspirational as I have. This book is practical, timeless and especially useful for entrepreneurs and job seekers alike. No matter where you are in your career, you will find some nugget that will help you develop better, stronger relationships. If you liked my books – *Never Eat Alone* and *Who's Got Your Back* – you will definitely enjoy this book.

Keith Ferrazzi

Introduction

The 5,000-square-foot Marquesa ballroom at the Montage Hotel in Beverly Hills, Calif., is Spanish Colonial-inspired, with grand chandeliers, opera balconies and lush draperies that are fit for billionaires, executives and celebrities. On this Saturday night in January, Oscar-winner Sean Penn has invited 300 friends to join him for his third annual Help Haiti Home fundraising gala to support his nonprofit, J/P HRO, which helps tens of thousands of Haitian earthquake victims. The event is presented by Giorgio Armani. You can smell the power in the room and taste the opulence in the air.

Hollywood director Oliver Stone and his wife are sitting 15 feet from me. CNN anchor Anderson Cooper is the host for the evening. Sean Penn announces that at the end of the gala there will be a surprise guest performance. Suddenly, U2 frontman, Bono, as well as guitarist, The Edge, and drummer, Larry Mullen, Jr., walk on stage. Everyone in the audience are delightfully surprised — which includes celebrities like Coldplay frontman, Chris Martin, his then-wife Gwyneth Paltrow, Julia Roberts and Charlize Theron. Camera phones are out and flashes go off like fireflies. Tweets are flying about this iconic rock band.

After U2 finishes performing, the crowd trickles into the foyer area directly adjacent to the Marquesa room. I walk up to Grammy-winning singer Usher and mention that I had a great time at his nonprofit event in Atlanta, Ga., a few years ago. Seconds later, he walks up to British actor Idris Elba with a beaming smile and they greet each other like old friends. As I leave the fundraiser to attend an after-party at a Hollywood Hills mansion, the first person I see waiting for his car at the hotel lobby valet is billionaire Tesla Motors and SpaceX founder and CEO, Elon Musk.

Here's your first piece of advice. If you want to meet "Big Gamers" — anyone in a position of influence you think is out of your league, including but not limited to billionaires, executives and celebrities — attend celebrity-related charity functions.

Your first thought might be: Chris, I don't have the money to go to charity events. And that's fine. Although there will inevitably be times where you will need to make an investment, one of the things I will show you in this book is how to find consistent ways to network at the highest levels without spending a fortune to do it.

In meeting Big Gamers, I've found that those who have fame and immense wealth don't need it, and those who need more opportunities don't have it. Oracle's former CEO Larry Ellison doesn't need another billion dollars to add to his net worth. But millions of Americans, if they had more personal and professional opportunities, could provide more for their families, send their kids to better schools and save up for their retirement.

The reason why the rich get richer and the poor get poorer is partly because rich and famous people regularly get to attend these types of charity events — so their wealth stays concentrated. Those at the top of their industries are aware of the best professional opportunities and, more importantly, have access to the power brokers who can get deals closed.

Maya Angelou so beautifully said, "When you learn, teach; when you get, give." I have attended thousands of networking events in hundreds of major cities while traveling a half-million miles around the world. What I have learned I want to share with you because I wish someone had already written this book when I started out.

MY STORY

Growing up, I lived a very modest lifestyle. I never attended any charity events where I could meet billionaires, executives or celebrities. I grew up in a middle-class home in Woodside, Queens. My mother was an elementary school teacher and my father was a case manager for the City of New York. I used to get hand-me-down clothes from my two older brothers and cousins.

My mother prepared my lunch every day. Gallantly, she attempted to make a version of hamburgers, using two slices of Wonder Bread instead of hamburger buns. When I opened up my lunch box at school, I'd press my fingers into the soggy bread and bite down hard on a crusty flavorless burger, trying my best to enjoy my mom's homemade cooking while my classmates wondered what on earth I was eating.

When I first moved to Los Angeles more than 10 years ago, I knew a handful of people but none of them were Big Gamers. The first few years of my consultancy business were painfully debilitating and discouraging; I was juggling being a consultant, author and speaker while still pursuing a singer-songwriter career. Whenever I visited my family in New York, I could hear the concern and worry in my mother's voice when she commented how thin I was. "Make sure you eat," she would remind me.

But that all began to change when I started focusing on meeting Big Gamers. After writing my first book, a college success guide to help readers understand how to pursue their dreams, all of a sudden, wealthy parents started hiring me as an educational consultant. They asked me to help their sons and daughters with their college admission essays and interview skills.

Over the years, I shifted to focusing on primarily corporate clients and large nonprofits, where my services ranged from business development, marketing, book publishing and speaking services. I also slowly assembled a team of business mentors who could complement my shortcomings. I chose mentors who were in my industry as well as leaders that were not so I could see problems from different perspectives. They became my shotgun and backseat drivers as I ventured off into the wilderness of opportunity.

Ignorance is not bliss. Self-awareness is bliss.

As an author, speaker, publisher and former singer-songwriter, I have published three books, given more than 1,000 speeches or workshops, both domestically and internationally, released a seven-song EP, had TV, radio and film song placements, and executive produced and co-wrote a corporate jingle that went viral worldwide.

To date, I have met or worked with numerous Big Gamers in professional and nonprofit settings that included: billionaires, multi-millionaires, heads of state, rock stars, celebrities and models, corporate executives, venture capitalists, private equity, movie producers, athletes, entrepreneurs, political and nonprofit leaders, law enforcement, school administrators and tech innovators in the U.S. and around the world.

The best and most purposeful use of meeting Big Gamers, however, is to help those less fortunate. Four years ago, I created Mondays at the Mission, the only homeless youth program of its kind at Union Rescue Mission, the largest private shelter in the nation.

Over the last four years, we have helped hundreds of homeless students stay in school, find jobs and attend college. Our program was mentioned on "The Ellen DeGeneres Show" and we have had more than 190 speakers from 23 states and 19 countries ranging from neurosurgeons to NAVY Seals, professional athletes to Grammy-winning producers. We have been blessed to have influential business icons like Atari and Chuck E. Cheese's founder, Nolan Bushnell, co-founder of MySpace, Chris DeWolfe, and Tesla Motors and SpaceX CEO, Elon Musk, as our guests.

I recognize that some of you might have no desire to meet a billionaire or celebrity. But if you want to have the best opportunities at your job or career, or you want to start your own business, then meeting executives at your company or in the field of your choice is paramount to your professional success.

According to an ABC News report in 2012, 80 percent of jobs people get are from networking.[1] And if you combine that with data from the Bureau of Labor Statistics, the median average tenure for a U.S. worker over 16 is only 4.6 years. If you are between the ages of 20 to 34, the average tenure drops down to 2.2 years.[2]

The question isn't, "Do you need to network?" We all know we need to. The question is, "Why do I need to network with Big Gamers?" When you know and understand what executives are thinking about, it allows you to plan and think through your career choices.

For instance, I have a friend who works at NRG Energy, Inc., a billion-dollar publicly traded energy company. NRG is dual-headquartered in New Jersey and Texas, although he works in the California office. He might not know or care that David Crane is the CEO, but having a chance to meet him and to understand the company vision from the CEO himself has tremendous value. Later on, if he decides to apply for a senior position at his firm, he will sound more knowledgeable, aware of where the company is heading and how he can add more value to the firm. If he doesn't proactively go out to network with Big Gamers, in this case with his CEO or senior executives, he will rarely get that in his day-to-day work duties unless he keeps track of companywide memos that may or may not share what direction the overall company is moving toward or macro-level industry trends. It's always best to get firsthand information from the source.

Start thinking like an executive and you will focus more on macro-, high-level issues. Thinking like an executive involves meeting the people who are leading the charge, finding the unique opportunities and knowing what pitfalls to avoid. Billionaires, executives and celebrities are the Big Gamers of their industries.

When you meet Big Gamers, you can learn new things and be inspired by what's going on in the world. Many of them have blogs, websites, books and interviews online and offline. For example, I check Bill Gates's website (gatesnotes.com) every day. Mark Cuban offers pithy and straightforward business advice on his Maverick blog.

After Facebook COO Sheryl Sandberg wrote *Lean In*, her website (leanin.org) filled with inspiring stories from female leaders. The Milken Institute Global Conference posts all their panel discussions online free for anyone to view. You can learn about how Charlize Theron is helping South Africa cope with AIDS or what doctors are doing to invent better, faster and cheaper medication.

Lastly, and most importantly, when you meet Big Gamers, you have the opportunity to find, work or volunteer with visionary leaders who are making the most impactful difference in the world. That's where celebrities and billionaires come in.

If you decide you want to make a lasting difference in a particular field, chances are very high that there are also celebrities that are passionate about that cause, too. If you are a strong advocate for the environment and attended an event organized by a nonprofit called Oceana, you might see director James Cameron or Leonardo DiCaprio at one of their annual fundraising galas — they are both passionate environmentalists.

At the 2014 Stanford University graduation, Melinda Gates was co-commencement speaker with her husband, Bill. She spoke about how she went to visit a hospital in rural India and met a woman who had AIDS. Because there is a deep stigma about AIDS in India, this woman was dying alone, a "pariah" to everyone around her. Melinda held this woman's hand and helped her fulfill a dying wish — simply to sit on the rooftop of the hospital to watch the mesmerizing sunset.

The main point is this: Strive for greatness by working with those around you who are doing big things. If you apply what I am going to teach you, I am confident that you will exponentially improve your chances of expanding your circle of influential friends, colleagues and collaborators. Though I'm referring to it as networking, it's really about creating a purposeful and powerful community of great friends and supporters in order to make a lasting difference in the world.

WHO SHOULD READ THIS BOOK?

This book is most useful for anyone in sales or business development roles, budding or seasoned entrepreneurs, those working at startups or nonprofits who want to raise funds, career changers, people who hate their jobs, thrill-seekers, celebrity enthusiasts or fans of Keith Ferrazzi's *Never Eat Alone* and Timothy Ferriss' *The 4-Hour Workweek.*

THE FORMAT

Time and time again, I've found that the endless parade of people I have met, from students and entry-level blue-collar workers to entrepreneurs and chief executives at multinational corporations, do not really understand, appreciate and know that networking, especially Big Game networking, must be learned, honed and perfected for you to create dynamic personal and professional relationships.

In 2007, billionaire Charlie Munger, who is also Warren Buffett's business partner, gave the USC Gould Law School commencement speech. Along with other priceless pearls of wisdom, he talked about how the easiest way to solve problems is to look at the problem in reverse. For example, if you want to help India, he said, don't ask, "How do I help India?" Instead, ask, "What's doing the worst damage in India, and how can they avoid it?"

So I won't ask you, "How can I help you network better?" Instead, I will ask you, "What are the 20 most common mistakes you are making in networking, and how can you avoid them?" Each chapter will offer advice about what you should do before, during and after an event.

This book is broken into four parts:

1. READY: A HIGH-LEVEL UNDERSTANDING OF BIG GAMERS

Big Gamers live in a different world. Remember in high school when you saw the prom king, head cheerleader or richest kid in the school walking around like they owned the world? Well, if you lived in their world, you might feel the same way. Big Gamers live like kings and queens.

2. AIM: BEFORE AN EVENT

Before you go and meet your first Big Gamer, invest the time to prepare yourself in the right way. There is a right and wrong way. The wrong way is doing no preparation. We will talk about the right way.

3. FIRE: DURING AN EVENT

Once you are at an event, Big Game networking is not a spectator sport. You participate or you lose. Winners take consistent action. Losers make excuses of why they can't do something. I believe you are a winner.

4. RE-LOAD: AFTER AN EVENT

Have you ever attended a networking event, met many interesting people and collected a stack of business cards, only to have them piling up on your desk, gathering dust, just a week later? Stop the madness.

Success is in the follow-through *after* an event. You waste so many countless hours meeting people at events if you don't follow up. Learn how to create a simple system to track who you meet and develop a community of Big Gamers.

Many of the things I suggest are obvious and common sense. If I were to encourage you to be healthy, we all know you should eat well, exercise regularly, get adequate sleep and drink a lot of water. But how many of us actually do it? For meeting Big Gamers, you want to focus on researching who they are, building confidence to approach them and learning how to be a great listener to understand how you can best help them.

So much of life isn't about learning new things; it's about re-learning old things in a new way. But, most importantly, it is about applying what you know consistently, intentionally and purposefully every single day of your life. Knowledge is not power; applied knowledge is power. When you read through my book, imagine if I am writing 20 handwritten, large, bright, scented, florescent yellow Post It notes to remind you how to develop great relationships so you can live a more fearlessly fun and ferociously fulfilling personal and professional life.

Aim high. It is worth it.

Section One

Ready: A High-Level Understanding of Big Gamers

"The greatest danger for most of us is not that our aim is too high and we miss it, but that it is too low and we reach it."
—Michelangelo, Italian painter and sculptor

ONE

10 Feet From the President

I remember very clearly when I began writing my first book. I was a 22-year-old recent college graduate who had just moved into my first apartment, a 400-square-foot converted basement apartment in College Point, Queens that cost me $400 a month. In my living room I had a TV, coffee table, sofa, one fold-up table and chair. In my bedroom, I had a twin-sized bed and a small wooden desk. I was sitting on a brown metal fold-up chair as I stared at my computer screen and typed my book title, *Your Wonder Years: Success in College and Beyond.*

It was my first place, so I really didn't care that I had such sparse furniture. I felt free and independent, which was the best feeling in the world. By that point, I had already begun jotting down notes for a book I'd wanted to write three years earlier, when I was a sophomore at the University at Buffalo. In college, I was often frustrated with myself. I would spend hours poring over my textbooks, wondering why I couldn't absorb the material fast enough, and then feel extremely frustrated when I would take tests and not do as well as I had hoped. My grades did not represent the level of effort I put in. I thought to myself, *Why hasn't someone written a college guide to help people like me?*

I knew that I wanted to find successful individuals to contribute to my book, so I reached out to my college professors and local politicians and asked them what career advice they would give to college students. As I began thinking about who else to write to, I thought to myself, *Why not aim higher?* So, I wrote to New York Mayor Rudy Giuliani. The more I thought about it, I realized I might as well ask New York State Attorney

General Dennis C. Vacco and New York Gov. George Pataki, as well as Vice President Al Gore and President Bill Clinton. *I have nothing to lose*, I thought.

I received replies from all their offices. They were form rejection letters saying how they appreciated that I wrote to them but unfortunately the person I was contacting was too busy to personally respond. Still, it was quite exciting to open my mailbox and see an actual envelope from the White House or the vice president. I did manage to receive a real response from then-New York State Attorney General Vacco, the second highest-ranking elected official in New York State.

Eighteen years later, when I attended the Clinton Global Initiative Annual Meeting, I sat 10 feet from Clinton when he was being interviewed by CNN Talk Show host Erin Burnett. I haven't yet met Clinton, but by that point I had met Gore and President Barack Obama.

The point of my story is that ever since I received that letter from Vacco, it proved to me that if you aim high, even if you don't hit your mark, you will achieve far more than had you just settled for what's in front of you — a target you know you can reach. I have always kept that "I have nothing to lose" mentality.

What I have added to that statement is a "there is so much more to gain" mentality. When you seek out Big Gamers, the one quality you develop most is courage — not the absence of fear, but the ability, tenacity and strength to push through your fears, to live the life you can only imagine in your dreams. Each time you aim high and do your best to engage a Big Gamer, you eventually become a more confident, determined and ambitious individual.

TWO

Profile of a Big Gamer

As we discussed in the introduction, I define a Big Gamer as anyone in a position of influence that you think is out of your league. The most challenging Big Gamers to meet are billionaires, Fortune 500 executives and A-list celebrities. If you are extremely ambitious and you envision yourself to be a national or global leader, then this section is especially important and pertinent to you. When you can better understand their lives, the lessons you learn in this book will help you engage them.

The five main distinctions of a Big Gamer are:

1. THEY INHABIT A DIFFERENT WORLD.

Melanie is a romance novelist. She likes to spend her afternoons writing in her office in Woodside, Calif. She reads The Wall Street Journal and The Economist. She gets her nails done at Susan's Nails in Menlo Park, works out three days a week at the Axis Performance Center with personal trainer Scott Norton, prefers Hermes handbags (an alligator Hermes bag can cost $29,000) and drives a two-seat Mercedes SL-55 AMG (base price of $113,000).

She met her husband, Larry, at Bix Restaurant in San Francisco. At the time, she was in a nine-year relationship — and engaged. Larry was persistent. Even though Melanie was taken, Larry would invite Melanie and her fiancé to various events. When things didn't work out with her fiancé, Melanie decided to give Larry a chance.

Their first date was for a muscular dystrophy benefit. Eventually, they got married. As a couple, they'd eat at Gaylord of India and Su Hong in Menlo Park. For fun, they'd fly to Malibu on the weekends or go yachting.

Melanie is Melanie Craft, billionaire Larry Ellison's former wife. I read about her typical day in a San Francisco Gate article written more than 10 years ago.[3] (At the time of the article they were still married, although they have since divorced.)

If you break down her story, Melanie lives in Woodside, one of the most expensive neighborhoods in the country, prefers $29,000 Hermes handbags, dines at expensive restaurants and goes "yachting" for fun.

It's a *different* world.

2. EVERYONE WANTS A PIECE OF THEM.

John Paul DeJoria is the co-founder of Paul Mitchell hair care products and The Patron Spirits Company. When I attended one of John's speeches a few years ago, someone from the audience asked him how many charities approach him for donations. John said that he has about 200 charities a month that ask him for help. He and his wife pick about a dozen to support. Two hundred. In one month. That's a lot of charities. In fact, there are more than 1.5 million nonprofits in the nation.

If you are a newly minted lottery winner with $100 million, what are the first things that will happen? Everyone around you — your family, friends, coworkers, colleagues, acquaintances and people you haven't spoken to in years — will suddenly want to know how you are doing, probably with their hand outstretched asking for help, like in DeJoria's case.

3. THEY ARE ONE-CALL BALLERS.

Journalist Lisa Ling and her sister Laura co-wrote *Somewhere Inside: One Sister's Captivity in North Korea and the Other's Fight to Bring Her Home* in May of 2010. In this book, they write about the harrowing ordeal that both of them faced while Laura was a prisoner in North Korea and Lisa was working tirelessly to try to get Laura out of prison.

On one such day, Lisa got a phone call from a restricted number. She didn't answer the phone. Then, she received an email from President Obama's office telling her that the president was trying to call Lisa and that she should pick up the phone.

When Lisa finally picked the phone, Obama reassured Lisa that he and the U.S. government were doing their best to resolve this issue so that Laura and her coworker Eunice could return safely home.

Lisa Ling is an example of a one-call baller. She is literally one call away from the president of the United States or other influential Big Gamers. Very few people in the world can pick up the phone to call (or in this case, receive a phone call from) the president of the United States.

During the process of helping her sister, Lisa was not only just one call away from Obama, she also reached out to some of the most powerful leaders in the world, like Gov. Bill Richardson, then-Sen. John Kerry, former Vice President Al Gore and former President Bill Clinton. Clinton would be the person that eventually traveled to North Korea to successfully secure the release of Laura and Eunice.

4. THEY ARE GLOBAL CITIZENS.

Stephen is a serial entrepreneur. He regularly travels between Los Angeles, New York and Chicago to organize functions to meet and develop deeper friendships with his colleagues and collaborators. In the same month, he was in both Dublin, Ireland for Web Summit 2.0, dubbed "the Davos for Geeks," and London, England.

Big Gamers travel a lot. According to William D. Chalmers, the author of *America's Vacation Deficit Disorder*, although less than 5 percent of 300 million Americans travel overseas, roughly 60 percent of all high-net-worth individuals go on five or more business trips a year and 34 percent take 10 or more business trips a year. Thirty-three percent of these individuals take five leisure trips per year and 11 percent of them take more than 20 leisure trips a year.[4] You need only look at the Twitter feeds of Paris Hilton or Bill Gates to learn about their world travels.

5. THEY HAVE AN ENTOURAGE OF HANDLERS.

A black stretch limousine pulls up outside the front door of the Four Seasons Hotel in Beverly Hills, Calif. A stocky man in a suit walks up and opens the back door. Out walks billionaire Sheldon Adelson, one of the honored guests at the evening's charity event. As soon as he steps out of his limousine, he sits down in a motorized cart and drives forward, flanked on all sides by his security detail as he rolls past me.

The more powerful and wealthy the Big Gamer, the more handlers they often employ. Whether they have a security detail that follows them around or simply an entourage of assistants, managers, talent agents, public relations consultants, lawyers, financial advisors, family members, business partners or friends, someone is usually there to protect and shield them from the public. When I met Scooter Braun, who is best known for discovering Justin Bieber, he passed me off to his assistant. When I emailed his assistant, I found out his assistant had an assistant.

THREE

Warning — Keep Out

American Express is a multibillion-dollar Fortune 500 company headquartered at Three World Financial Center in downtown Manhattan, across the street from the World Trade Center. Founded in 1850, it is a financial services corporation most known for its credit and charge cards. As of 2013, American Express had 63,000 employees.

More than a decade ago, I used to be an American Express employee. I started off as a compliance analyst at American Express Bank at 7 World Trade Center; I was promoted to be a business strategy and communications manager in their corporate services division at 40 Wall Street. I felt like they valued me as an employee and individual and that they had very approachable executives.

After leaving my job at American Express, I sold my 18th floor apartment in a luxury high-rise in Forest Hills, Queens, and moved to San Francisco to finish writing and self-publishing my first book, *Your Wonder Years: Success in College and Beyond.*

Once I finished a strong rough draft, I knew I would need testimonials from prominent individuals, so I thought that the next time I was in New York I would ask Kenneth Chenault — then American Express' COO, although he would soon become the CEO — to consider it.

The next time I visited New York, I asked a friend and former coworker who still worked at American Express to give me a security-access card into the World Financial Center. My goal was simply to take my first draft of my book, give it to the receptionist to pass off to Mr. Chenault, and then be on my way.

What actually happened is what happens often: your life doesn't work out the way you planned it. After entering the World Financial Center building, I keyed myself through their turnstile on the ground floor and proceeded to the elevator to ascend to the floor where the chief executives had their offices.

As I got off the elevator, I proceeded to the reception area as planned and spoke to the security guard. "Hi, I'm Chris," I said. "I'm a former American Express employee. I wrote a college success guide and I just wanted to leave my manuscript here for Mr. Chenault and see if he could write a testimonial for me."

Without even acknowledging my question, the security guard replied, "How did you get access to this floor?" I fumbled with my words. "Ah, I asked my former co-worker to lend me his access card." He wasn't convinced, since normal employees would not have access to the most restricted floor of the building. "Sorry, sir. Like I said, I used to be a former American Express employee. I am just going to leave my manuscript right now for Mr. Chenault and walk away."

He raised his left arm and held out his hand, "Hold on right there. You're not going anywhere. Do not move! I am calling security from downstairs to escort you to our security office for further questioning. *Do not move.* Stand where you are."

With his stern warning, I realized the severity of my seemingly naïve actions:

1. I was trespassing on private property.
2. I had breached their security at the most restricted area on the premise.
3. I had a security-access card to the most restricted area on the premise.
4. My friend was unauthorized to give me this security-access card.
5. My friend could be fired for giving me this security-access card.

I waited nervously. The only two thoughts I had in my mind were: I am going to be arrested and my friend is going to get fired. I felt terrible. Finally, moments later, another stern-looking security guard walked off the elevator and asked me to follow him down to their security office.

When I entered their security office, I breathed a sigh of relief as he introduced me to his supervisor — who I had known when I was an employee. He looked at me rather surprised, wondering what I was doing there. As I explained the whole situation to him, he just smirked. "Chris, don't do that again, please," he finally said. He briefly chided me and said that he'd have a talk with my friend as well.

Thankfully, my friend did not get fired and I did not get arrested.

What I should have done was to simply write an email asking a senior executive I knew to forward my request to Mr. Chenault.

In your pursuit of Big Gamers, although you might have good intentions, it doesn't mean the people you approach will see them. They might only see you as a threat, nuisance or irritation. Remember, they get approached hundreds, thousands or — if they are really famous — millions of times each day, week or year. Don't take their lack of interest in you personally.

I believe you can successfully network with Big Gamers. You *can* cold call or walk up to a Big Gamer you don't know, but ideally you should find someone who knows them personally who can make an introduction.

Section Two

Aim: Before an Event

"New beginnings — professional, personal or come what may — are always uncomfortable, but being open to them is the only way to grow. In the end, we are all capable of so much more than we think."

—Marissa Mayer, President and CEO, Yahoo

FOUR

Know Your Why

Ray Dalio is the founder of Bridgewater Associates, the world's largest hedge fund. He is also one of Time Magazine's "100 Most Influential People." He wrote a book called Principles (which you can download for free at bwater.com), in which he shared his five approaches to getting what you want from life. In his first approach, he talks about how you want to work for what you want, not for what others want from you.[5]

The most fundamental question you have to ask yourself is why you want to meet a Big Gamer. Be crystal clear. For instance, if you are an entry-level analyst and the Big Gamer you want to meet is the vice president of your department, ask her what specific steps she took to become vice president. If you are working a 9-to-5 job but you want to start your own business, ask numerous entrepreneurs in your field of interest what specific steps they took to get started. If you are struggling financially and you meet a millionaire, ask her specifically what types of weekly, monthly and annual goals she used to achieve her financial success.

Whenever I approach a Big Gamer, what I want falls into three specific categories. I ask these simple questions:

1.) *Business*: Can they be my mentor, strategic partner or potential client?
2.) *Charity*: Can they inspire my class of homeless students as a speaker?
3.) *Friendship*: Are they interesting enough to be my friend?

I have generally found that I lead with the second — charity — because it gives them an opportunity to serve a specific cause and helps me build a community of altruistic friends. Lead with what works for you. Try different approaches, but make sure you are clear, concise and compelling with your ask. If you are in a situation where you can actually have a conversation with them as a warm up, that's great. If not, you may have one quick attempt to ask one good question.

If I want to meet a corporate executive for a business mentorship, I'll say, "Hi Doug, I really admire your business success. I know you're busy, but can I take you out to lunch once a month to learn from you?" If I meet a celebrity or billionaire who I want to come speak to my students, I'll say, "Hi Elon, I created a homeless youth program and I'm always looking for speakers. If I emailed you my information could you consider coming to inspire my students?" And, for friendships, I might say, "Hi Lisa, I really find you to be an interesting person. Could I take you out to coffee sometime?"

All of these are actual asks that worked. Doug is a successful corporate executive that owns a portfolio of 105 restaurants in 13 states serving 7 million customers. After I asked him this, he became one of my mentors and eventual clients. Elon is Elon Musk, the billionaire entrepreneur that started Tesla Motors, SpaceX and PayPal. He came to speak at my homeless youth program. And Lisa is Lisa Ling, the pioneering journalist who I ended up having coffee with.

KEEP IT SIMPLE

1. Start with a compliment. Then ask your question.
2. Rehearse and record your ask out loud. Make it less than 10 seconds.
3. Try different asks. Use the one that works best.

FIVE

Give Them a Reason

Have you ever gone to a job interview, nervous and afraid, but as soon as you walked into the room and sat down, your interviewer greeted you with a firm handshake and warm smile, making you feel as if you had been close friends for years? This is the ideal to strive toward.

The reason that interviewer is warming you up is so she can ask the questions she needs to ask to see if you will be the right fit for the open position, the team and the overall company.

When you first meet a Big Gamer, give them a reason why they should stay in touch with you. How do you stand out from everyone else they meet? You have to give them that reason. Be that warm and welcoming interviewer that asks the right qualifying questions to see how you can help them. Train yourself to be a keen listener. For someone like myself who likes to talk a lot, there are numerous times I consciously have to take a deep breath when I feel that I am talking too much. The next time you are in a conversation, consider just listening. Don't have a question ready to ask before they finish their sentence. Take more deep breaths.

Focus on the most common denominators. In conversation, just start with three basic things. For example, you could ask about where they grew up, why they are at the event and which interesting person they have met so far.

When you listen, pay attention not only to what words are spoken but also to how the person expresses their words and what subjects they talk about. For instance, if you're having a conversation with someone and for

80 percent of the conversation they are talking about their five-year-old daughter, don't change the subject and talk about sports.

Talk and ask about their interests. If they don't seem very open, share your interests with them to develop a deeper connection. As Stephen R. Covey wrote in *The 7 Habits of Highly Effective People*, seek first to understand, then to be understood. In some instances, you might not have more than 10 seconds to talk to them, so keep in mind that the understanding might have to be quick.

After getting to know someone, continue with these three things:

1. BUSINESS OPPORTUNITIES

No matter which Big Gamer I have met — be it a billionaire, corporate executive, entrepreneur or celebrity — the majority of them are open to business opportunities even though they could have retired yesterday. Make sure you present them a credible business opportunity that's interesting at their level of play. Remember, you are talking to Big Gamers, so they are likely not interested in rabbit-sized opportunities.

For instance, I have a friend who wants to acquire and operate an existing business that grosses $10 million to $50 million in annual revenue. If you were to approach him with a startup idea or a movie project, he wouldn't be interested — it's not in his line of vision. Know who you are pitching and pitch at their level of interest.

If you are a startup that wants to raise money, Guy Kawasaki, a venture capitalist and former chief evangelist at Apple, suggests following a 10-20-30 pitch.[6] Make your pitch 10 pages long, with 20 font size, and present for no more than 30 minutes. Consider reading "Elements of an Enduring Company" and "Writing a Business Plan" on the Sequoia Capital website.[7] They have invested in numerous companies, including Google, Apple and Twitter.

2. CHARITY

There are many Big Gamers who support charities or have started their own. A few years ago, business titan Richard Branson tweeted that anyone who would donate $2,000 to his charity would be invited to meet him at a private party in Miami Beach at the Versace mansion.

Seventeen-year-old aspiring entrepreneur Stacey Ferreira saw that tweet and immediately responded to Richard's message.[8] She told Richard that she wasn't even old enough to drink yet but that she would love to meet him, support his charity and share a new business idea. Richard responded and invited Stacey and her brother to meet him. With just a few days' notice, Stacey convinced her parents to foot the bill, and she and her brother flew to Miami and met Richard Branson. He ended up investing $400,000 in her startup called MySocialCloud.com, which is essentially a password storage space in the cloud.

I recognize that $2,000 or even $200 can be a lot of money. But as I said in my introduction, sometimes you will have to make that investment. You are donating to a great cause and it is one of the best ways to meet or work with a Big Gamer because you are showing them with your wallet that you care about what they care about. Refer to the "Power of Free" section if you really want to attend these charities without a monetary donation.

3. MENTORSHIP

Max Talmey unknowingly changed the world forever. When he was a 20-year-old medical student, he started mentoring a 10-year-old boy named Albert. Over the course of five years, Max would meet Albert weekly for lunch. Max recognized the genius in Albert and gave him his first science books, taught him math and introduced philosophy to him. His precocious student would end up changing the course of the world with his understanding of physics. His name was Albert Einstein.

Einstein once said, "If you judge a fish on its ability to climb a tree, it will forever think it's stupid." How many of us think we are stupid in certain areas, especially if we did not do well in school? In high school, although I did well academically, I performed horribly on my SATs; I felt like I was an idiot. Thankfully, even before I took the SATs, I had my Uncle Ding. He was my first business mentor, starting from the age of 12 when I worked at his insurance company to bolster my confidence.

Ask Big Gamers if they can be your mentor. Although they are incredibly busy individuals, make it easy for them to say yes. See if you can meet once a month for lunch. If that doesn't work, ask them for a monthly phone call. If that still doesn't work, see if you can just stay in touch via email from time to time. Any help is better than no help. Always be appreciative of their time.

KEEP IT SIMPLE

1. Ask questions to learn about Big Gamers' interests.
2. Find mentors: They are your carpool lane to success.
3. Ask yourself: How can I help this person?

SIX

Research the Big Four

Dr. Marco Curreli has two passions in his life: nanotechnology and education. Originally from northern Italy, he completed his Ph.D. in chemistry, with an emphasis in nanotechnology, at the University of Southern California in Los Angeles. His goal is to inspire and educate American students to focus on careers related to STEM fields — science, technology, engineering and math. Marco decided to create a nonprofit organization called Omni Nano, which offers manuals, books, presentations and lesson plans to teach high school students about the exciting field of nanotechnology that is already revolutionizing the world.

When I first met Marco, I was impressed with his commitment to education. I suggested that he learn about Dr. Patrick Soon-Shiong, a pioneering surgeon, biotech entrepreneur, billionaire, chairman of the Chan Soon-Shiong Family Foundation and passionate advocate of nanotechnology.

He found out these interesting facts about Dr. Patrick Soon-Shiong:

1.) *Who is he*? Patrick was born in Port Elizabeth, South Africa, although he is of Chinese heritage. He graduated high school at 16 and medical school at 23, studying at the University of British Columbia and doing his surgical training at the University of California at Los Angeles. Today, he's married with two children.

2.) *What does he do*? He is a pioneering surgeon, biotech entrepreneur, philanthropist, chairman of his family foundation, professor at UCLA, minority owner of the Los Angeles Lakers and the chairman and CEO of NantWorks, LLC.

3.) *How did he succeed*? He founded and sold two biotech companies valued at almost $10 billion.
4.) *When can I meet him*? He started the annual Innovation Awards. This event is hosted by the Los Angeles Business Journal and recognizes innovative tech companies in California. Patrick likes to call his awards the "Oscars for Geeks."

When you research a Big Gamer, focus on the Big Four: 1) Who they are, 2) What they do, 3) How they became successful, and 4) When you can meet them. While researching the Chan Soon-Shiong Family Foundation, Marco learned that there were only two people on the board of directors: Patrick and his wife, Michelle B. Chan. Since it was a relatively new family foundation that did not accept unsolicited grant proposals, the only way to get their attention was to meet them in person.

I had attended the Innovation Awards before, so I forwarded Marco's information to Patrick's director of public relations. At the same time, a friend of Marco decided to nominate his organization for an award. Omni Nano was ultimately chosen to be one of the 15 finalists at the Innovation Awards in 2014, becoming the first ever nonprofit to receive this honor. At the awards ceremony, Marco met Patrick and his wife. Today, he is in discussions with their team to see how they can work together.

Whoever you want to meet, it has never been easier to learn about Big Gamers. Focus on the Big Four by using Google search, as well as LinkedIn, YouTube, Facebook, Instagram and Twitter. Don't forget to check the person's personal blog or website, as well as company or nonprofit websites. When you do your research like Marco did, you will have the best chance to meet and work with Big Gamers.

KEEP IT SIMPLE

1. Focus on the Big Four.
2. Know them better than you know your best friend.
3. Find shared interests.

SEVEN

Meet 'Those' People

I used to live in Arcadia, Calif., a tree-lined suburban town 19 miles east of downtown Los Angeles. One afternoon, I was lying in the pool in the backyard; in an adjoining house, I heard loud music from my neighbors' house — they were clearly having a party. I had just moved in, so I decided to jump out of the pool, change and walk around the block to meet my neighbors.

Since it was a party, the door was open. I walked in and started talking to a middle-aged woman in her 50s. Most of the attendees were much older than me. Everyone there looked like they were family members. It turned out to be an 80th birthday party for a guy who looked like George H.W. Bush.

The party was full of people I might have considered "those" people, folks who might dress, look or think differently than me, with dissimilar political views. But when I walked in, I just told them I was their neighbor and that I had just moved in, so I decided to come by to say hi. I ended up having a great conversation about tennis, art and travel with the daughter of the grandfather whose birthday it was, as well as a few of her family members.

If you're Christian, meet Muslims. If you're a man, go hang out with a group that's predominantly women. If you're in your 20s, meet people in their 30s, 40s, 50s and 60s. If you're a Baby Boomer, mingle with Millennials. If you're Latino, network at an Asian-centric function. If you're straight, meet more gay friends. If you're deeply religious, talk to an atheist. If you're a teacher, go to a business-related event.

Jack Ma was an English teacher before he created the Chinese company Alibaba, the largest e-commerce business in the world — one that had the largest Initial Public Offering in U.S. history. Before he became the richest man in China, as a teenager in his hometown of Hangzhou, he would ride his bike for 40 minutes to a nearby hotel to practice his English with foreigners. He would give free tours of his city to these English-speaking tourists, where one of them gave him his English name, Jack. Unlike many successful Chinese entrepreneurs who studied in the U.S., Jack had no money, connections or status. What he did have was a strong and fierce desire to learn from other people.[9]

When you are able to meet and hold in-depth conversations with a variety of different people who don't look, think, dress or act like you, every person you meet will be like a university professor teaching you something you don't know. This ability to learn and grow as a student of life will give you an immeasurable level of confidence to approach and speak with Big Gamers.

KEEP IT SIMPLE

1. Attend at least one event each month with different types of people.
2. Meet three new friends at these events.
3. Learn about new cultures by asking specific questions.

EIGHT

Create Your Shared History

A few years ago, a former elementary and high school classmate named Noel called and left me a voicemail. He lives on the East Coast with his wife and kids but heard that I had moved to Los Angeles. He was traveling to Las Vegas and wondered if I might be in the area. I hadn't spoken to Noel in more than 15 years, but we had attended the same two schools in Queens for 12 years of our lives, and he was one of my best friends growing up. I immediately felt a deep sense of nostalgia.

When we had attended St. Mary's Elementary School in Woodside, Queens, both of us were fiercely competitive and hyper-energetic. I remember countless summer days playing handball, tennis and riding go-carts in Noel's vacation home alongside our good friend Charlie. He and I were also the shortest kids in our class. When we graduated from St. Mary's and attended Archbishop Molloy High School, an all-boys school at the time, all of our freshmen classmates towered over us. I was only 4' 10" going into high school.

Even though we did not speak much in high school or college, when I heard his voice that day, I was immediately transported back to our rambunctious childhood. I ended up canceling my plans that day and drove four hours to Las Vegas to meet him. Over dinner, we reminisced about all our childhood adventures, friends we still kept in touch with, and what we're doing with our lives since we last spoke.

Noel and I have a shared history together as childhood friends. I'm sure you can remember your own special moments with a childhood friend. History — a personal shared history — between two individuals is the difference between a casual acquaintance and a more meaningful friendship.

Do your best to create meaningful friendships and start creating your own shared history with Big Gamers. Contact them before an event and tell them how much you admire them — be specific — and that you are excited to meet them in person. When you meet them, you will be more of a familiar face than the nameless sea of faces at the same event.

Sometimes, you won't be able to find their contact information even after looking at their business and nonprofit websites, LinkedIn, Facebook, Twitter or Instagram accounts. Other times, you would be surprised how easy it is to get a Big Gamer's email. For instance, if you wanted to raise money for your startup and wanted to contact a partner at Sequoia Capital, one of the most well-known venture capitalist firms in the world, look on their website — everyone on their leadership team has their email listed. No one is stopping you from contacting them.

And don't just contact them in one way. You can't assume they are checking any of their accounts regularly, so if you have their email, Facebook and Twitter accounts, contact them in as many ways as possible to increase your chances of engaging them before an event.

Build your shared history today.

KEEP IT SIMPLE

1. Reach out to them at least a week before an event.
2. Reach out to them in as many ways as possible.
3. Be specific about why you want to meet them.

NINE

When Opportunity Knocks Loudly

Live Talks LA (livetalksla.org) hosts phenomenal speaking events throughout the year in the Los Angeles area. The first one I attended was a conversation between author Ben Mezrich and Hollywood mega producer and director Brett Ratner, who directed "Hercules," "X Men" and the "Rush Hour" movies. Mezrich is the author of two books that were both adapted into movies — *Bringing Down the House: The Inside Story of Six MIT Students Who Took Vegas for Millions*, which became the film "21," and *The Accidental Billionaires: The Founding Of Facebook, A Tale of Sex, Money, Genius, and Betrayal*, which became "The Social Network."

When I arrived at the William Turner Gallery at the Bergamot Station in Santa Monica, there were only about 80 people in the audience — many were USC film students. I couldn't believe it. Normally, for such high-profile speakers, there are more people and a steeper ticket price. When I realized it was going to be such an intimate event, I texted an actress I had recently met to tell her about this great opportunity.

Here is our edited text conversation:

Me: X Men director Brett Ratner is speaking tonight at 8 p.m. at Bergamot Station. It's only $20. Come if you're free. Order tickets at livetalksla.org.

Actress: Hi Chris, I wish. I never miss my acting class unless I'm in a movie or something really important like that.

Me: That's the point. This IS important. You have two of Hollywood's most powerful directors and writers in one room with only 80 people. You could meet both of them and get their contact info.

Actress: Yes, but I'm not at their level yet so I'm not ready to talk to them. That's why I'm going to school. I want to be confident in front of these people and have my 30-second pitch ready. I need just a little more time.

Me: That's not how life works. You meet them whenever the opportunity comes. Say hi. They probably won't remember you. Then you meet them again, and over time you build a rapport.

Actress: I understand. It was too short notice.

She never came. I ended up meeting Ben and getting his email. I briefly met Brett, but more importantly, sitting in the audience, I met one of Brett's executives — who has worked with him for 15 years. I also met another established director in the crowd. I invited all of them to my homeless youth program as speakers.

Just because you go to meet one Big Gamer doesn't mean you won't meet others; you will often find their friends in the audience, offering you more opportunities to meet other Big Gamers you didn't plan on meeting.

Sometimes opportunities like this one knock very loudly. There are many reasons you can tell yourself not to take them: You're not ready; you don't feel like going; you're scared; it's too "last minute." So you say no, rather than taking a leap of faith and saying, "Absolutely, yes!" You only grow when you stretch yourself. What works for building muscle flexibility works for learning how to be more courageous. If you have a 9-to-5 job, I recognize that being flexible with your time can be challenging and very impractical. Do what you can, especially on weeknights and weekends. But always remember, when someone is pounding on your door with an opportunity, simply take a deep breath and open the door.

KEEP IT SIMPLE

1. Opportunities can happen at any time.
2. Be bold and let the moments unfold.
3. Don't always stick to a schedule. Be spontaneous.

TEN

The Power of Free

Big Gamers get premium access to the best events, but they come at a price. The more exclusive charity galas can cost hundreds or thousands of dollars per ticket. The original TED and Milken Institute Global Conferences both cost $8,500. The pinnacle of world power and influence is the World Economic Forum in Davos, Switzerland — it costs $52,000 to be a member. You can also pay to join any number of private country clubs and private membership groups. For example, Tiger 21, a high-net-worth investor group, has a $30,000 annual membership fee. If you do not have the budget right now to attend these events, here are five proven and tested ways to get in for free.

1. VOLUNTEER

Before you consider paying for an event, consider volunteering at it. Not only can you get into the event for free, you also have an opportunity to meet the organizers before the event so you can build deeper friendships with the people running the show.

Since charity events exist to benefit nonprofits, many nonprofits are open to having volunteers because they need the help. One drawback of attending as a volunteer is that you might get stuck in one area where you do not have any interaction with Big Gamers. For instance, if you're stationed at a door to welcome guests, the guests just walk by you. But if you're a volunteer usher, you have more opportunities to strike up a conversation. You ideally want to find volunteer positions that allow you to walk around the event as freely as possible. The other drawback is that every event is so different, meaning some organizers treat you like a dignified human being while others treat you like an expendable sheet of toilet paper.

What you might not realize is that even high-profile Big Game events recruit volunteers. The Clinton Global Initiative Annual Meeting actively recruits volunteers about a month before the event in August. The ticket price is $20,000, but if you volunteer, it's free. I highly recommend attending, even if you do not live in New York; it is one of the most inspiring events I have ever experienced — imagine four days of ambitious do-gooders that are changing the world, one commitment at a time.

Focus on a cause near to your heart. If you are passionate about our oceans, volunteer at oceana.org. If you love pets, help out at peta.org. If you want to advocate for more AIDS research, get involved with amfAR. There are more than 1.5 million nonprofit organizations in the U.S. — find one that aligns with your purpose.

Don't know what cause you're passionate about yet? Visit looktothestars.org to find a list of high-profile celebrities and the nonprofits they support. Whatever the organization, simply visit its website and contact it about volunteering.

2. PRESS PASS

Any high-profile event featuring celebrities will have a red carpet and a crowd of press outlets covering the event. The larger and more well-known the event — like the Academy Awards or Grammy Awards — the more press will be there to cover the event. Although established publications like Variety and The Hollywood Reporter still cover these events, with the increasing number of online media outlets, there are numerous blogs and websites that now gain premium access to many Big Game events.

For example, Jared Eng is a celebrity blogger who created www.justjared.com. His blog gets over 80 million views per month and is so well known in Hollywood that he has become a mini-celebrity himself. He regularly gets invited to many of the A-List celebrity events.

If you can write, take photos or videos, or interview well, consider becoming a freelance producer, writer, host, photographer or cameraperson and look into getting a press pass from a traditional news source — or start a blog like Jared did. The best way to identify what press outlet to approach is to think about what you read — and the best place to contribute is to one you already know, inside and out. If that doesn't work, attend a few charity events or any press-related function as a paid guest or volunteer and during the red carpet portion (generally an hour before the start of an event), walk up to some of the press there — not the household names. Find the one that is least known. If they got in, you can, too. Whichever media outlet you decide to approach, make sure you have sample work you can show them.

A year ago, I reached out to Look to the Stars, a website that highlights celebrity charity news. I simply emailed the editor to see if I could cover events for them. It worked. I have served as a freelance producer and correspondent for a number of Big Game events. Sometimes, you will be invited only to cover the red carpet where you get to interview celebrities, but there are many instances where they allow you into the main events.

3. BE THE +1 GUEST

Look to your most outgoing friends and see which ones attend Big Game events. Next time they attend an event, ask them if you can go as their +1 guest. And don't give up if they say no the first time. Ask them periodically. Once you start attending Big Game events, you will start to see similar faces. Don't be shy in making new friends. As long as you ask politely, being assertive is much more effective than *hoping* you are asked to attend.

Attend a Big Game event with your most outgoing friend with the specific purpose of meeting other very outgoing people at these events. Once you stay in touch with these outgoing individuals, start inviting them to events that you get invited to, and ask them to reciprocate.

4. LOBBY HUGGER

We have all heard of tree huggers. I encourage you to be a lobby hugger. This might surprise you, but if you cannot get a press pass, be a volunteer or be invited as a guest, if you simply just stand around in the lobby of a conference or charity event, you can meet so many Big Gamers that are simply walking by or having a drink at the bar. In just the lobby area at the Sheraton Time Square hotel in New York during the Clinton Global Initiative, I met a Greek billionaire; I met Jimmy Wales, the founder of Wikipedia; I met a private equity executive, a startup entrepreneur, and Nobel Peace Prize winner Muhammad Yunus.

It might seem silly to be standing around a lobby if you aren't a registered attendee at the event, but if you actually did attend some of the larger conferences, you'll find many executives doing the same thing — they know it's the best way to connect with fellow Big Gamers all at one time. They often set up meetings in the lobby or in dining areas with friends or other attendees. If it is a full or multi-day conference, the best times to go are during lunch and dinner, or immediately after dinner when there is the most foot traffic. As long as you dress the part, you can mingle with the crowd.

If you are not comfortable meeting Big Gamers yet, go to the closest five-star hotel and sit in the lobby area. Watch and observe the people there. Observe their age group, gender, race and ethnicity, what clothes they are wearing, who they are with and how they carry themselves. The more comfortable you get seeing them, the more confident you will become when you meet them.

5. PROFESSIONAL OR BUSINESS DEVELOPMENT

If you work for a client-based firm like a bank or insurance company, you can always just ask your boss if the company can reimburse you if you attend a specific Big Game event where you can meet prospective clients. Most professionals recognize the value in attending events that draw a more affluent audience.

KEEP IT SIMPLE

1. Find a local nonprofit you believe in and ask to volunteer at an event.
2. Research how you can get a press pass.
3. Look at all free options before paying for an event.

Section Three

Fire: During an Event

"Go to places where business contacts are likely to be. And try to cold-call people out of the blue. I got a couple of summer jobs that way. Just go out and try to meet as many people as possible."

—Elon Musk, founder and CEO of SpaceX and Tesla Motors

ELEVEN

Your Safari of Success

In Swahili, the word "safari" means "journey." Your future journey with Big Gamers is directly related to what types of charity and non-charity-related events you attend. Most people network at the wrong events. They attend events with their friends or colleagues who are at the same level of employment. If you attend an event with mostly entry-level workers, you will have entry-level job opportunities. If, however, you are an entry-level employee and attend executive-level events, you will have Big Game opportunities.

Also, stay away from free events unless a Big Gamer invites you. If the event is free, then anyone can attend. The more people that attend, the more people want to meet the same Big Gamer you want to meet.

CHARITY EVENTS

The first time I rubbed elbows with Paris Hilton was at a Brent Shapiro Foundation event in May 2008. Robert Shapiro, the famed attorney for O.J. Simpson, was hosting an annual "Sober Day" event to highlight the dangers of drug and alcohol abuse in honor of his son Brent, who tragically died of drug-related causes in his 20s. The party was held at the Palazzo di Amore, a 25-acre estate in Beverly Hills owned by his real estate developer friend Jeff Greene. In recent years, Rockstar Energy Drink was one of the sponsors on the red carpet.

This one event had the seven main criteria that will determine whether you will meet Big Gamers at charity events:

1.) *Celebrities*: The more A-list celebrities that have attended past events ensures the highest probability they will attend again. Sometimes, charity events say they are presenting Brad Pitt an award, for instance, but it doesn't guarantee that Brad Pitt will attend. If you go to more established charity events that have proven that they can draw celebrities, that is a better bet. Focus on who is headlining the event. Big names draw Big Gamers.

2.) *'Bill' and 'Mill'*: When it is affiliated with a BILLionaire, there will be other Big Gamers there – especially, if the billionaire is also a celebrity like Virgin Group CEO Richard Branson. MILLionaires will also be there because many of them aspire to be billionaires.

3.) *Location*: Having a luxurious location is one of the best indicators of whether a Big Gamer will be there. If a Big Gamer is accustomed to living in mansions and dining in expensive restaurants, they also like to attend events in places they are used to going to.

4.) *Red Carpet*: One of the main points of a charity function is to draw attention to the cause. Having a red carpet and an invited list of A-List celebrities ensures greater exposure. The amount of press that covers an event is directly related to the amount of celebrities and their level of fame.

5.) *Sponsors*: Focus on billion-dollar or luxury brands like American Express, Louis Vuitton or Gucci. The biggest brands draw the biggest names. These types of brands are not interested in reaching a small amount of people. They invest premium dollars to reach millions of viewers. That's why they sponsor these events in the first place.

6.) *Exclusivity*: The more exclusive, the better. Focus on invite-only or high price-point events. Big Gamers like to be treated well. Why would they go to events that everyone knows about and can attend? Remember, if you were in their shoes and had all the choices of events to attend in the world, wouldn't you be very selective as well?

7.) *Quality over Quantity*: As a general rule, the more intimate the event, the better. Focus on the quality of the people attending, rather than the number of people that show up.

A great website to find these types of events is guestofaguest.com if you live in Los Angeles, Washington D.C., the Hamptons, New York and Miami. If you don't live in these cities, find similar type websites that focus on more high-end events. Again, focus on the well-to-do Beverly Hills-type areas.

For example, here is a step-by-step process about how I might find events with the highest chance of Big Gamers. Recently, I went on guestofaguest.com and identified one specific event:

3RD ANNUAL PLACE AT THE TABLE EVENT

When I visited the heifer.org, the organizer of the charity event, they were honoring Tom Colicchio, Lori Silverbush, Annie Griffiths, Diane Lane and Ian Somerhalder. At first glance, I only recognized actress Diane Lane. But, what most peaked my interest is that it would be held at the Montage Hotel in Beverly Hills. The Montage is a fancy hotel in Beverly Hills which costs a lot of money to rent the space, so I was sure it would be a good event.

After researching the other honorees (since I don't watch TV) I didn't know that Ian Somerhalder is a famous actor and has 5 million Twitter followers, Tom Colicchio is the head judge on Bravo reality TV show "Top Chef," Lori Silverbush is a director and producer and also Tom's wife, and Annie Griffiths is a famous photographer. And, the ticket price was $500.

This is a specific example of a Big Game event. It has celebrities, a premium location and a steep ticket price. Though I don't know if there are any billionaires or who the sponsors are, three of the seven main criteria are enough for me to decide that it is a worthwhile event.

NON-CHARITY RELATED EVENTS

The most useful events to meet business executives will have a large or majority percentage of its attendees that are Big Gamers. For example, at GMIC, a global mobile technology event in Silicon Valley, 56 percent of the attendees are executives.[10] If you were interested in entering the mobile technology market, this would be an excellent event.

Tech Week Los Angeles is an annual event that draws many executives in the startup world. It's another event that clearly lists the types of attendees on its website.[11]

1.) 39 percent make over $100K annually
2.) 53 percent are management level or higher
3.) 34 percent are senior-level executives

ACCESS POINTS

Once you have narrowed down what events you want to attend, the usefulness of the event comes down to one thing — access points. Can you actually get to talk to Big Gamers? In the case of the charity function where I met Paris, you could since it was in a very large outdoor dining area. If you attend certain conferences or awards shows, the Big Gamer is on stage and never mingles with the people off-stage. You want to find the type of events where you can meet and befriend Big Gamers. That is why charity events are great — there is usually a small group of people mingling in a cocktail, dinner or after-party setting.

WHERE TO START

For business-related events, local chambers of commerce and business journals have the most upcoming events in your area. Bizjournal.com has 43 cities across the country you can research. Find your city and note the events that most interest you. If you can't find your city or any events on this website, do a Google search for your city name and "business journal" to see what events are available.

Depending on the specific chamber of commerce or business journal, you may or may not find many Big Gamers there. Do your research. Two organizations that focus only on business Big Gamers are the Entrepreneurs' Organization and the Young Presidents' Organization.

The Entrepreneurs' Organization has more than 10,000 members in 142 chapters in 46 countries. The Young Presidents' Organization has more than 22,000 members in 400 local chapters in more than 125 different countries. YPO and EO both have specific age and revenue requirements, but even if you don't meet the requirements, find out who in your area is a member of YPO or EO and see if you take them out to coffee or attend one of their events.

Here is an email I sent to a YPO member in my area:

Hi Gary,

I just moved to the Westside from the Pasadena area. I am originally from NYC. I saw that you are involved with the YPO Malibu chapter.

As a sales and marketing consultant (one of my niche services is writing books for executives), I do not meet the YPO requirements yet, but I wanted to see if I could be invited as a guest to one of your YPO events, or perhaps we can meet for coffee.

I'd like to connect more with ambitious, intelligent and service-oriented people to build a team to live our dreams.

Thanks,
Christopher Kai

For the most ambitious of you — those who want to work on the world stage — four of the most premier events and their organizations are:

January: World Economic Forum in Davos, Switzerland

March: TED conference in Vancouver, British Columbia

April: Milken Global Institute Conference in Los Angeles, Calif.

September: Clinton Global Initiative Annual Meeting in New York, New York

Not only do these organizations host an annual flagship event, they also host events and communities you can participate in throughout the year. For example, the Milken Institute not only has a California and London summit but also has industry-specific events like the Partnering for a Cure conference. If you wanted to make an investment you could be one of its Associates or Young Leaders.

KEEP IT SIMPLE

1. Find the most densely populated events with the most Big Gamers.
2. Focus on local events with global leaders.
3. Walk before you soar — but start now.

TWELVE

The Ideal Profile

Although I have been nurturing a community of influencers for years, I had never used the term "Big Gamer." The term didn't occur to me until a few years ago, when I was talking with one of my mentors Fred Joyal, a successful business owner based in Los Angeles. When I asked him how I could best scale up my business, he simply said, "Don't be shooting at rabbits, if you want to hunt 'Big Game.'" He was essentially telling me to look at the clients I wanted instead of the clients I had. If I wanted larger clients with a much greater potential for growth, then I had to focus on finding "Big Gamers" — corporate executives, in my case — that had larger budgets to hire me as a consultant.

Put simply, the Big Gamer you want to *meet* is the person you want to *become*. If you are a writer and want to be a published author, your Big Gamer is a published author. As we discussed in the introduction, if you are an employee but want to start your own business, your Big Gamer is an entrepreneur. If you want to become a millionaire, your Big Gamer is a millionaire. We have already talked about "Know Your Why" and "Research the Big Four"; now, it's time to go even deeper.

The three types of people you most want to meet are:

1. THE OBVIOUS ONES

The obvious ones are the headliners, the big names who draw the crowd. For any conference or fundraising gala, if the big names include Brad Pitt and Bill Gates, those are obvious people you want to meet. The obvious ones are also sponsors and organizers. The organizers somehow succeeded in getting the Big Gamers to show up, so meet the organizers. Sponsors are who bankrolled the events, so meet them as well.

When you are at a charity event, the center tables closest to the stage are generally where the VIPs are seated, which would include the sponsors and awardees. The exception to that is, if the entire event is very intimate with only a few hundred people. In those cases, the position of the table might not mean as much. I attended one charity dinner where Academy Award-winning director Oliver Stone was on one end of the room while Julia Roberts, also an Academy Award-winner, was on the opposite end.

2. THE LESS-OBVIOUS ONES

I see this happen all the time. The celebrity is swarmed by their fans, while there is a person who is with the celebrity that everyone ignores. Usually it's their date, family member or one of the handlers I mentioned in my first chapter.

The less obvious ones are who the Big Gamers know. If you stand away from the Big Gamer and just watch and observe them, look very closely who walks up and talks to them on what appears to be a more intimate, personal level. This is not an exact science but *birds of a feather really do flock together*. Just because you don't know who the Big Gamers are talking to, you can take the initiative to meet his/her friend.

I attended a music event last year, where Maroon 5 frontman Adam Levine was receiving a lifetime achievement award. He was seated with a table of 10 people. Every person that sat at his table would constitute as a "less-obvious-person to meet." You have a much better chance of working with the Big Gamer in the long run if you first introduce yourself to his inner circle.

3. THE HARDEST TO CRACK

So, what if the Big Gamer is not on the press list, nor do you see anyone that is talking to the Big Gamer. How do you find Big Gamers then? This is where the quality of the event comes into play regarding how exclusive the event is or isn't.

The seemingly simple answer is to approach someone who looks important. They wear nice clothes and look the part. (I will talk about that in the "Be Denzel" section.) The less simple answer is just because they look the part, that doesn't mean they are Big Gamers.

The only way to find out is by approaching them and asking qualifying questions. When I was a singer-songwriter, for instance, one of my qualifying questions was, "Do you know who Dr. Luke or Max Martin are?" If they said, "No," I would realize they weren't serious about breaking into the music business because they didn't know the two most successful commercial music producers in the world. It's like you saying you want to be the best basketball player and you don't know who Kobe Bryant or Lebron James are.

The people you most want to avoid are the excessive talkers with no substance, gossipers and pessimists. They will drain you. If you end up talking to someone who doesn't seem focused on your conversation, and it's hard to keep his focus, those are very frustrating people to speak with. When you talk to people who gossip or are always focused on the negative aspects of life, they are putting their own self-imposed handcuffs on their future opportunities. Of course, there are Big Gamers that fall into each of these categories, so you will have to decide if they are worth your time. Perhaps you're attending an event where Oprah Winfrey is the headliner; she's who you want to meet. Everyone there probably wants to meet her, too, so it'll be challenging. Instead of just focusing on the headliners, focus on creating an ideal profile of other Big Gamers you want to meet.

Perhaps it would look like this:

Occupation: Media executive
Net worth: $10+ million
Industry: Entertainment
Years of Work Experience: 10 years minimum
Competencies and Skill Sets: Business savvy and great speaker
Location: Chicago
Age: 35-55

Now, instead of just wanting to meet Oprah, you have other potential Big Gamers that you could meet at the same event. The more specific you can get, the more targeted your events will be. At the actual event, when you meet someone, if they fall into your ideal profile, you can decide right then and there if you would like to continue the conversation.

For the most part, it's actually a lot like dating. Whenever we meet someone new, we often take mental notes on their qualities; based on these qualities, we decide if we want to date them. In this case, you can decide whether you want to follow up with them or not. You can spend so much time wondering what events to attend and whom to approach — but it's a frustrating endeavor if you don't know whom you want to meet. If you spend more time to research and create your ideal profile, you will have a clear focus on who the Big Gamer is you want to meet and eventually work with.

KEEP IT SIMPLE

1. Focus on what Big Gamer you want to be like.
2. Create your ideal Big Gamer profile.
3. Be selective with who you meet.

THIRTEEN

The Three-Second Rule

Once you have thought through what you want and how you might help a Big Gamer get what they want, don't hesitate. How many times have you seen someone that you wanted to talk to at an event and hesitated? You started thinking: What should I say? What if he doesn't want to talk to me? I don't want to bother him.

Use the "three-second rule." When I see someone I want to talk to, if I wait more than three seconds to approach them, I have already waited too long. Hesitation kills dreams. The only way to break inertia, inactivity and complacency is by action. The more you wait and think about what to say, the harder it becomes. If you just start by walking up to them, you'll end up in a conversation.

If you are meeting a Big Gamer at a high-profile event where you might only have a chance for a 30-second dialogue, just politely ask for what you want, or how you can help them with what they want.

One of the most common questions I get asked about approaching Big Gamers is, "Chris, what do I say?" Remember, no matter how rich or famous someone is, they are still human beings. They wake up in the morning, brush their teeth, eat breakfast and go to work.

It really doesn't matter how you begin a conversation. I like to start with a smile. I say, "Hi, I'm Chris. How did you hear about this event?" You'll know after asking that one question what their demeanor is. Do they look annoyed or distracted? Are they folding their arms in a defensive posture? Or, do they have a look on their face that says, "I don't want to be bothered"?

If they respond cordially and are friendly, you can try to start a conversation. I might ask two more questions like, "Have you met anyone interesting here yet?" Or, "Are you originally from this area?" If they don't reciprocate by asking you any questions, or just give you one-word answers, you probably won't be having much of a conversation. Just politely say, "Nice meeting you. Enjoy the event" and walk away.

The only two reasons why you should wait to talk to a Big Gamer is if you don't know who the person is and you have to do some quick research on your smartphone, or if they are talking to someone else — which they usually are. In those cases, survey whether it looks like an intimate conversation between two very good friends, or if it looks like the person is talking to someone they just met. Watch their mannerisms and body language. If you were talking to a close friend, you might lean in more and perhaps smile at each other or hug. If it seems like an intimate conversation, wait for them to finish and then make your approach.

If it seems like they are having a casual conversation, walk up beside them, forming a triangle between the two people, standing so they clearly see you. Either jump into the conversation when appropriate, or wait your turn. Be tactful, polite and professional.

Even if it appears rude to jump in, if you smile when you introduce yourself, that one smile can pave the way to an inclusive conversation. If they didn't want to talk to new people, they wouldn't be at a networking event.

For conferences where you want to meet the headline speakers, approach them before they get on stage. (I always have a photo of them on my phone so I know what they look like.) I recently attended a tech conference called the Be Great Festival at the Los Angeles Design Studios. The closing speaker was a seasoned entrepreneur who has raised hundreds of millions of dollars for startups and had over a billion dollars in exits (which is when a company is sold to a larger business). Although there were hundreds of people walking around, I was the one stranger who recognized him, so I walked right up to him and struck up a conversation. We spoke for a solid 10 minutes.

After his captivating speech, a crowd of 20 people waited patiently in line to meet him. While others were waiting to talk to the speaker, I found his wife in the audience and started talking to her about both their professional and personal lives. The next time I see him, I will already know his personal story, business experience, his wife and two son's names, and even their pet dog's name.

Remember, don't overthink things. It's not about you; it's about them. Focus on them. I hear all the time from friends who hesitate; they say, "Chris, I don't want to bother them." If you begin your approach thinking that you're "bothering them," you begin with a defeatist mentality. That's not a good start. Think about how you can add value to the conversation and to their lives. Ask questions and genuinely be interested in what they are saying.

KEEP IT SIMPLE

1. Don't wait. Start walking toward them.
2. Action is the only way to break inertia.
3. Keep it simple. It's not about you; it's about them.

FOURTEEN

Bring the Right Set of Wings

Larry Gagosian is not a household name you'd recognize unless you're in the blue chip art world. In 2011, the British magazine Art Review ranked him as the fourth most powerful person in the art world. He is the Kobe Bryant of art dealers. Although he has 11 gallery spaces in major cities like New York and London, during Oscar season, he hosts an annual exhibition open to the public at his Beverly Hills gallery.

During the annual exhibition, I had a friend visiting from Barcelona who had said he wanted to meet more influential people. So I decided to invite him. But when he arrived, I saw that he had brought a date. The fact that he brought a date prevented him from meeting new people; furthermore, his date became upset about something, so they left early. Though he did see actor Edward Norton, he missed out on a great networking opportunity.

It can be helpful to bring a wingman or wingwoman to help you meet Big Gamers, but you have to bring the *right* person. Don't bring a friend or date unless they can help you network more effectively. The friend you bring should help you better understand who the Big Gamer is or help present you in a better fashion.

If you can't find a friend like this, you are better off going to events alone and learning how to network better. When I network alone, I often meet more people, build more courage and have more conversations.

You already know that when you go with certain friends, you end up talking more with them than with anyone new. Our friends can be very reliable crutches. It's easy to stand there and talk to your friend. You feel comfortable.

You don't want to feel comfortable. You want to leap out of your comfort zone. That's how you build courage to meet Big Gamers. Courage is like a rubber band. The more you use it, the more it expands.

KEEP IT SIMPLE

1. Attend at least one networking event by yourself each week.
2. Leap out of your comfort zone.
3. Find the right wingman or wingwoman.

FIFTEEN

Timing Is Everything

The best time to network is anytime you can. There are two types of networking: 1) Casual and 2) Professional. Casual networking is when you go out with your friends, co-workers and colleagues with no specific intention of networking. You're just spending quality time with your friends, or meeting new ones. You don't even consider it networking.

Ideally, you can meet friends that become co-workers or colleagues, or vice versa. This is just the go-with-the-flow mentality. It works well if you have friends that are Big Gamers or know Big Gamers. If your friends are mostly at your current level of employment, then this casual approach might not be very helpful.

Professional networking is going to an actual networking event like a lunch, dinner or conference with the specific purpose of meeting new clients, colleagues or contacts. The more prominent the Big Gamer, the bigger the potential opportunity. In these instances, start the very moment you step out of your car, train or plane and continue as you make your way to an event.

The reason this is so helpful is that everyone is slightly nervous when they attend new events. You don't know who you're going to meet and perhaps you feel unprepared; maybe you had a bad night's sleep the night before, or maybe you rushed to get to the event, forgot to eat and are now starving. But if you just casually start talking to people on the way to an event, when you arrive, you'll have already made a new friend or two. You are warmed up and ready to go.

Whether you just parked your car and are walking to the venue, in line waiting for your coffee or sitting at the lobby lounge waiting for your colleague, if your purpose in attending a conference or event is to meet people, meet them where they are — literally. If you are on the shy side, I recognize that this can be painfully awkward or hard, but it doesn't have to be. Think of each person as a potential new friend and treat them as such — as a friend. If they are not friendly, just walk away.

So much of my networking with Big Gamers happens before, in between and after scheduled events. For example, if you attend a dinner, once you sit down, you are sitting with the same nine people at your table. But you really only get to talk to the person sitting to your left or right. It's more challenging and at times awkward to talk to the person across from you. Sitting at a table is very restrictive and limiting — unless, that is, you are sitting directly next to the Big Gamer you want to get know. In that case, it's perfect. But that's rare.

Consider networking when you're in the following places:

1.) Waiting outside restrooms
2.) In and near valet parking areas
3.) In hotel lobbies
4.) Walking through venue hallways
5.) Walking in parking lots
6.) Riding inside elevators
7.) Waiting in any line, anywhere
8.) At the reception before the event
9.) On the red carpet before the event
10.) At parties held after the event

I met a film producer as we both waited in line at a charity event. He ended up using one of my songs in his film and helped give me the chance to work on my first independent film as a production assistant and an assistant director. At the beginning of another charity event, I met a business executive that has been one of my largest corporate clients.

KEEP IT SIMPLE

1. Spend more time meeting people than listening to speakers.
2. Approach Big Gamers anywhere you can.
3. Warm up by talking to someone new right before an event.

SIXTEEN

Be Denzel

One of my favorite films is "Training Day" starring Denzel Washington as a corrupt cop training a new recruit played by Ethan Hawke. He delivers such a strong commanding performance based on his choice of words, tone/feeling and body language. As a viewer, you believe him.

THE WORDS

Every industry has a basic jargon that you should learn. If you are a musician, you should know how to talk about chord progressions, playing out or song structure. If you are in business, you should know basic terms like market capitalization, emerging markets or revenue streams. If you're in the startup space, basic terms might include unique value proposition, profit margins or exits.

If you don't understand the most basic terms in your desired industry, it's like you're trying to be an architect without understanding how to read a blueprint. Spend the necessary time learning the language of the trade and you will eventually speak the part.

TONE/FEELING

Although this might sound awkward, I suggest you record yourself in front of a mirror pretending to introduce yourself to a Big Gamer. Just keep it simple. Say two things — your name and, "It's nice to meet you." So I would say, "Hi I'm Chris. It's nice to meet you." Watch the video and ask yourself: "If I can't even say my own name with a firm, crisp tone, how will anyone — much less a Big Gamer — believe in me?" Practice. You will get there. Speaking well is a learned skill.

BODY LANGUAGE

Here's a simple exercise to develop strong body language. Stand with your back to a wall, with your upper back (both shoulder blades) and both heels touching the wall. Walk away from the wall and stand in front of a mirror — you want to be able to see yourself in a full-length mirror. Stand with most of your body weight firmly back on both heels.

Now, look at your face. Smile at yourself. Does your smile look natural? Show some teeth. A genuine smile conveys that you are a genuine person. I know this exercise sounds so simple, but I still meet so many people that rarely smile, so they look grumpy, annoyed or irritated. Who wants to befriend them?

DRESS THE ROLE

A friend who works for an institutional investor once invited me to a nice restaurant in Century City called Hinoki and Bird. He had a friend who worked as a nonprofit development executive and I was considering how I might raise funding for my charitable work, so my friend decided to connect the two of us.

My friend arrived dressed in a clean, professional dark grey suit and collared shirt. His friend wore an elegant black dress. We all spoke about traveling, our corporate experience and philanthropic activities. We all dressed the part.

Whether we like it or not, many people do judge a book by its cover. Dress the part as best you can. You don't have to shop at expensive stores to look good. But do make an investment in a nice suit or dress and nice shoes. Even if you have a limited budget, buy what you can (and find a good tailor so that it fits well). If you do these simple things, you will feel more confident. Substance and style are a winning combination.

KEEP IT SIMPLE

1. Speak the language of your desired industry.
2. Be aware of your tone and body language.
3. Videotape yourself and objectively examine what you can improve.

SEVENTEEN

Approach With Unflinching Confidence

The key to approaching a Big Gamer is to project a deep sense of confidence. The best way to project confidence is by learning how to be a great public speaker. I encourage you to dramatically improve your public speaking skills by joining a local Toastmasters club. Toastmasters International helps its members improve their communication and leadership skills through public speaking. They have over 300,000 members in 14,650 clubs in 126 countries. In most cases, it costs only $36 every six months to join. It will be the best investment of your life.

You're probably thinking, "Chris, I hate to speak in public." Yes, most people do. That's why it's even more important to speak well. You'll gain an immeasurable level of confidence if you can excel at public speaking — and it's a crucial way to differentiate yourself from everyone else. Just because you have the intention to meet Big Gamers, if you don't have the skill set, you will never meet them. Luckily, these skills can be learned.

Another great hands-on approach is to take an acting or improv class. You might not feel confident — and no one ever does all the time — but if you can learn to act confident, anyone who meets you will perceive you as such; perception is reality. Just like actors snap into character when the cameras roll, you can train yourself to turn *it* on at any time. You always want to be prepared to meet Big Gamers.

Strip away the impressive titles, the Walmart-family-sized bank accounts and the over-inflated fame, if you were to meet Bill Gates, Marissa Mayer, Alessandria Ambrosia or Katy Perry tomorrow, they would still be just like you and me: living, breathing, in-the-flesh human beings.

And just like you and me, Big Gamers are either friendly, or they're not. If they aren't friendly, move on. It's not worth your time. Just because Katy Perry has 63 million Twitter followers, that doesn't mean she's a better person than you or me. She might be more famous and wealthy, but that doesn't say anything about her as a person or her happiness.

You must never confuse your value as a human being with your bank account value or any other exterior sign of success. If you value yourself as a human being, meeting a Big Gamer is simply meeting a new friend who happens to be wealthy or famous. If you start with that mindset, you can and will approach anyone, anywhere and at any time because you are equal in value as a human being to any Big Gamer.

Like anything, it takes practice. If you have never met a Fortune 500 CEO, billionaire or celebrity, the first time you meet one, you might start hyperventilating. But after you meet your second, third, fourth or tenth Big Gamer, you will see how truly normal and *human* they really are. They might be exceptionally talented, but they should not be idolized or put on a pedestal. The more you can treat them like a friend, the better chance you have of staying in touch with them.

Being confident or acting like you're confident doesn't mean you won't get nervous. Before I meet Big Gamers, I still get a little nervous and my pulse picks up — but feeling more alive and excited is a good thing.

KEEP IT SIMPLE

1. Join a Toastmasters club.
2. Take an acting class.
3. Don't look at your bank account to value your self-worth.

EIGHTEEN

The Treasure Chest

Paul Smith, author of *Lead with a Story: A Guide to Crafting Business Narratives That Captivate, Convince, and Inspire*, writes about a woman who walked into a Pizza Hut late one night in Arkansas. She asked the worker at the counter if they had meatball sandwiches; he said they did not. Since it was already late, the woman pleaded with the worker to make a meatball sandwich with whatever meatballs he had and some bread. It was the only thing her husband would eat, she said. After listening to this customer's plea, the worker relented and made a makeshift meatball sandwich with what he had. The woman thanked the worker effusively and left with her meatball sandwich.

The next day, the woman called Pizza Hut to speak with the same worker from the night before. She told the worker that her husband had late-stage cancer and that the meatball sandwich was the last meal he had — which he thoroughly enjoyed — before he passed away. She just wanted to call and thank him for his service.

Until Smith's book was published almost 30 years later, no one knew this powerful story of one woman expressing her gratitude for a complete stranger.

This kind of personal, heartfelt thank you is a treasure we can enjoy for a lifetime. Here are some of my treasures from past students I taught in high school and at a homeless shelter that I have kept with me through the years:

"You are a very rare and amazing person. I loved your class. For about three years I have felt like an outsider or like I would never amount to much but in your class you said I could do anything I wanted if I worked hard for it. I don't think I can ever forget you."

"You're truly an inspiration. You inspire me through your speeches and I really appreciate your honesty. Like every great speaker, you allow yourself to be at your most vulnerable state. I believe I've learned more about life within a week than I have within a year."

"I love that you're inspirational as a person, encouraging as a teacher and supportive as a friend. Your willingness to help others by opening up and sharing your past experiences, both positive and painful, is an attribute that is so rare and valuable. Thank you for sharing yourself with the world, your students and me."

If you meet a Big Gamer who deeply moves you, don't just say, "Thank you, you were amazing." Dig deeper: What did they specifically say or do that moved you? They probably hear, "You're amazing" all the time. But I am sure they will remember you if you tell them their speech changed your life. In a world inundated with texts, tweets and emails, if you were to write them a personalized, handwritten thank you card, that alone would leave an even stronger, more lasting impression.

KEEP IT SIMPLE

1. Buy a box of nicely crafted thank you cards.
2. Write a note including very specific details about how they helped you.
3. Include your contact information in the card.

Section Four

Reload: After an Event

"The fastest way to change yourself is to hang out with people who are already who you want to be like."
—Reid Hoffman, co-founder of LinkedIn

NINETEEN

As Bad as You Want to Breathe

Eric Thomas is known as the hip-hop preacher. Originally aired on YouTube, his speech "As Bad as You Want to Breathe" went viral, catapulting him to Internet fame. In this speech, he talks about a young man who meets a guru. He tells the guru that he wants to make a lot of money. The guru tells this young man to meet him at the beach the following morning at 6 a.m. The next morning, the young man meets the guru dressed up in a suit and tie. The guru says to the young man, "Come walk into the water." The young man thinks the guru is crazy — he doesn't want to ruin his suit. "You said you want to make money, right?" says the guru. "Yes, I do," the young man responds. The guru says again, "Come walk into the water." At first, the young man walks into the water where it is waist deep, then neck deep. Finally, he can barely keep his nose above water.

At that point, the guru dunks the young man's head into the water. The young man panics, gasping for air. When he finally emerges from the water, the guru says, "When you want something as bad as you want to breathe, you will get it."

It goes back to knowing your *why*. If you know your why — why you want to pursue your goal and what that goal is — your purpose will be deeply rooted. It's easy to get excited about attending a networking event. It's harder to find the right events and meet the Big Gamers you want to meet. But even after all your hard work of researching an event and meeting the Big Gamer, you waste so much time and money if you do not follow up. You have to want it *as bad as you want to breathe* — then you will follow up with the Big Gamers you meet.

Following up doesn't guarantee that you will succeed. But *not* following up will always end in failure and missed opportunities. Success is in the follow through. I ascribe to a 1-3-7 approach. Ideally, I follow up with someone I've met within the first day, the next three days or within a week. If you wait longer than a week, you'll lose the initial momentum of your meeting — that, and they may not remember you. We all lead busy lives. When you meet them for the first time, ask them directly, "What is the best way to follow up with you? By phone, email or text?" Never assume. Just ask.

Here are five simple ways to follow up and stay in touch:

1. 2 + 2 WEEKLY RELATIONSHIP GOALS

Angy Chin is the former CFO of The Coffee Bean & Tea Leaf. I met her through a client when she was the acting CFO and COO. We hit it off because she is a very passionate connoisseur of all things tea — and so am I. We both love authentic tea. Eventually, I reached out to her as a mentor; now, every few months, we meet to catch up.

During one such meeting, she spoke about how she has a 2 + 2 weekly goal of relationship building. Every week, she reaches out to two new friends to learn new ideas and two old friends to deepen relationships. I have since borrowed Angy's system and have found it to be extremely useful. It's just a unique way to say, "Hi, let's keep in touch." Whether you use a 1 + 1 weekly goal or 2 + 2 weekly goal, it's a unique way to stay in touch.

Here's a sample email:

> *Subject Heading: 2 + 2 Weekly Relationship Goals*
>
> *Hi,*
>
> *Great meeting you today! I have a 2+2 weekly relationship goal where I meet two new friends (to learn new ideas) and two old friends (to deepen relationships.) Would you like to grab coffee or lunch this week? It's on me.*
>
> *Thanks,*
>
> *Christopher Kai*

2. MONTHLY BLOGS

For 13 years now, I have written a private blog (before they were even called blogs) capturing what I call my Unique Life Experiences, or ULEs for short. It's called "The Adventures of Christopher Kai." I send it out every month to stay in touch with my family and friends, including some of the Big Gamers I consider friends. I don't include Big Gamers that I don't know very well — people get so many emails, so I don't want to assume they want to be included.

3. QUARTERLY OUTREACH

Try to reach out to your Big Gamers a minimum of once a quarter to see if they can meet or speak on the phone. Some of them aren't open to a meeting or phone call. The key is to let them know that you are thinking about them. Aside from following up with potential business opportunities or collaborations, focus on three simple things:

1.) *Introductions*
2.) *Education*
3.) *Entertainment*

If you have done your research, you should know what types of people they want to meet and what inspires them. When Google's Executive Chairman Eric Schmidt was giving a speech in my area, I invited one of my clients to join me, knowing that he would be interested in what he had to say. If you see a moving TED video, send it to a Big Gamer to inspire them. If you have an extra ticket to a sporting event or film, invite them. Let them know you are thinking of them. They will remember your generosity. As author Stephen R. Covey liked to say, you are making emotional deposits into your relationship bank account. Over time, all these deposits help to create a strong relationship.

4. ANNUAL TREATS

Call people on their birthdays, holidays or anniversaries. Take them out to coffee, lunch or dinner; buy them a gift if your budget permits. You can post a Happy Birthday message on Facebook or send a quick text or email, but that is all passive. You want to stand out. You want to develop an actual relationship, not a stream of text messages or emails. You should only revert to emails and text messages if those are the communication channels that have worked best in the past and you already know that the Big Gamer is not free to meet you. Whenever possible, always call or meet them in person.

5. CONDOLENCES

If something tragic happens to someone you know — like someone close to them passing away — reach out to them and let them know you care. It's easy to find friends to celebrate with you. But the real, true friends are there during your darkest or uncertain moments like a death, divorce, job loss, health challenges, catastrophic events or even simply unforeseen circumstances. For instance, although Sept. 11 happened more than 13 years ago, I still remember the first two people who called me that morning — my cousin Asa and my friend Yvonne.

KEEP IT SIMPLE

1. Follow up within a week of meeting a Big Gamer.
2. Follow up at least once every quarter.
3. Focus more on face time with a Big Gamer than Facebook.

TWENTY

Be a Hurdler

Kevin Olusola is a talented cellist and a member of an a cappella group called Pentatonix. Their YouTube channel has more than 800 million views and they are signed to RCA, a major record label. Kevin was the opening instrumentalist at one of the annual TED Conferences in Vancouver.

After his performance, he made a few contacts that he wanted to stay in touch with. Even though Kevin was one of the headliners, when he texted them a few times he didn't hear back.

You never know why a person doesn't respond; don't assume it's because they don't want to talk to you. Most of the time, it's because they are very busy. Remember, a Big Gamer might meet a few dozen or a few hundred people every week and get hundreds or thousands of emails each day. If you were in their shoes, would you remember everyone you met?

How many times have you attended an event, met a few interesting contacts, looked them straight in the eyes, and said, "Let's meet for coffee next week"? But then that coffee meeting never transpired. The reasons are many. Perhaps because something more pressing at work came up. You had a deadline. Or perhaps you had a friend visit from out of town and your schedule filled up for the week.

I just met a potential strategic partner at the Rosewood Sand Hotel in Menlo Park, Calif., a popular place for venture capitalists. I texted him the next day to tell him how great it was to meet him. I got no response.

Five days later, when I called him up, I found out that his uncle was near death and his father was sick, too.

If you don't follow up a number of times, you will never know the real cause for a person's silence. Don't assume.

That being said, if you don't hear back after a few times, knowing when to move on is as important as being persistent. How much you persevere depends solely on you. When you network a lot, especially with Big Gamers, you will get rejected a lot. I'm not talking about a few times or even a few dozen times. I'm talking about hundreds or thousands of times. Don't take it personally. Focus on the fact that you at least attempted to engage them. Change your mentality from asking, "Will I ever network with Big Gamers?" to asserting, "I will work with Big Gamers one day." The only question you will have to ask then is when and with whom.

No one likes to be rejected. You can look at rejection in one of two ways. The first way to deal with it is by taking it personally; it hurts, like you are slamming your head against a brick wall. The other, more helpful way is to look at rejection like it's a life hurdle. Every time you encounter a rejection, you jump over it like a hurdler. With each rejection, you become more resilient, strong and determined; you are a track star.

KEEP IT SIMPLE

1. Don't give up if you don't hear back right away.
2. Follow up at least three times within the first month after meeting a Big Gamer.
3. Be patient. If you attend enough events, you will meet them again.

TWENTY ONE

The Power List

If I were to give you $1 million in cash right now, what is the first thing you would do? You would probably drive to your local bank and deposit it, right? You'd make sure you put it in a safe place.

Well, your Big Game contacts are just as valuable as that money. But instead of thinking of it like cash, think of each Big Game contact you meet like a stock investment. Over time, these contacts might reap you returns, like Google and Facebook did for early investors. As you get better at meeting and vetting Big Gamers, you will refine who you want to meet and for what reason.

There are two simple ways to keep track of your Big Gamers.

1. MOBILE RECORD

Invest in a smartphone if you don't have one already. The first thing I do immediately after meeting a Big Gamer is to put their full name in my phone and note the date and place I met them. When I met Paris Hilton, for instance, I wrote "10.21.10 URM." I met her on October 21, 2010 at the Union Rescue Mission in downtown Los Angeles. You want to note their full name so that when you return home, you can learn as much as you can about them. When you follow up with them, you will be much better prepared to understand how you can help them.

2. THE POWER LIST SPREADSHEET

Once you return home, I suggest you log more detailed information about them. I keep an Excel spreadsheet called "The Power List" where I write down and track every single person of value I have met at networking events. There are thousands of people on my list.

You only need to know a few things: their name; why you want to contact them; when you first met them; the "progress" or status" of your follow up; their contact information; and a short profile that describes who they are. Include their race, gender, age, company name, position and details about their interests — or whatever you find interesting about them. In the references, attach web links to articles, videos or websites that help you better understand each person.

The two areas you want to update most are the "progress" and "profile" columns. Every time you communicate with each person, you want to learn more about their profile as well as what they are up to, which you can log in the progress column. Make sure you put details about your conversations. It will help you build rapport with them. Since success is defined in years, not months, weeks or days, it is so helpful when you can just pull up this list and know exactly when you last corresponded with them and what you talked about.

Most people in a sales role will use some form of CRM (Customer Relationship Management) software like Salesforce, ACT or Basecamp to help them keep track of any emails and correspondences. Do your research. Personally, I like to keep it simple and free. This Power List works for me. Use what works best for you. The most important lesson is to have a clear system of tracking the Big Gamers you meet where you can write notes and keep track of your conversations via emails, texts or phone logs.

KEEP IT SIMPLE

1. Create quick notes on your smartphone immediately after meeting a Big Gamer.
2. Create more detailed notes when you return home.
3. Create and update your Power List.

TWENTY TWO

Nurture 10-Year Relationships

Stephen Meade is a serial entrepreneur, author, speaker and investor. He has always impressed me with his ability to befriend Big Gamers. Stephen keeps three C's in mind when networking: Credit, Contacts and Compensation. Give people credit when they do something for you, be generous with your contacts and compensate them fairly when you can.

If you were to receive an email from Stephen, who is the CEO of Big Bamboo, LLC, his signature would read:

> *Why Bamboo? No, not because we sell Bamboo. It's an analogy that growing companies is like growing bamboo trees, and both offer a great metaphorical lesson. Unlike normal crops that you can harvest annually, the Chinese bamboo tree takes a little longer. The process goes like this: You take a little seed, plant it, water it and fertilize it, and nothing happens for four years. Then, sometime during the fourth year, the Chinese bamboo tree sprouts and grows 90 feet in six weeks! The story of the bamboo tree is much like growing a company — you have to have faith, belief and persistence.*
>
> *Additionally, it is a story of stability, structure and maturity. It's about laying down and growing the roots that will become the foundation to support massive growth.*

Although Stephen is talking about growing companies, you can easily fill in Big Game relationships in place of companies. Growing your Big

Game relationships is like growing bamboo trees — it takes time, patience and perseverance. And instead of a four-year life cycle, I think in terms of 10-year relationships. When I meet a Big Gamer, I ask myself, "Can I see myself being their friend in 10 years?" If the answer is yes, I stay in touch. If the answer is no, I move on. It saves you so much time, energy and effort when you think this way.

KEEP IT SIMPLE

1. Can you imagine a 10-year friendship with this Big Gamer?
2. The most meaningful relationships are deeply rooted.
3. Be patient. Everything takes longer than you think it will.

TWENTY THREE

Community First

Ken Rutkowski is a serial entrepreneur, radio host, keynote speaker and technologist. Originally from Chicago, when he moved to Los Angeles more than 10 years ago, he said that in his first few years in town, he kept meeting what he called "$30,000 millionaires." They dressed the part, wore the right clothes and drove fancy cars, but they were just putting up a front. They weren't millionaires and had no deal flow — they were just talkers.

He decided to start his own TED-like community and called it METal International, which stands for media, entertainment, technology and alpha leaders. Every Saturday morning, he hosts more than 100 entrepreneurs to learn from a keynote speaker. He also hosts weekly Sunday hikes and has a nationally syndicated radio show called Business Rock Stars. These three interconnected communities help Ken meet and befriend Big Gamers on a consistent level.

Start where you are. We have already discussed YPO and EO, but look at communities that you are already a part of: your neighborhood, ethnic groups, athletic, women or men's groups, member's-only clubs, alumni associations, Chambers of Commerce, nonprofits, political affiliations or special interest clubs. In an entrepreneur.com article, billionaire Richard Branson suggested "to get started, attend industry events and meet key players; join regional business associations and start learning about local market conditions. You can [also] meet potential mentors at schools, clubs and business groups."[12]

The key is to focus on a community first. Find or create communities where you can attend consistently — weekly is ideal, but aim for at least a few times a month or quarter. Keep in mind that in order to make it a Big Game networking opportunity, there have to be Big Gamers in the community.

The best relationships are those that happen organically, when you meet as friends and then, over time, find mutual career, business or philanthropic opportunities. In these communities, you feel less pressure to "network" for results and can focus more on developing friendships and living an inspiring life.

KEEP IT SIMPLE

1. Find and join consistent communities.
2. If you can't find one, create your own.
3. Meet regularly to develop deeper relationships.

Conclusion

"If you want to do the most, you have to go see the worst. In the course of your lives, you'll see suffering that's going to break your heart. And when it happens, don't look away from it. That's the moment change is born."
—Melinda Gates, co-founder of the Bill & Melinda Gates Foundation

An eight-year-old girl named Hannah forever changed my life. On Thursday, Sept. 2, 2010, this girl ran up to me and asked a simple question, "Do you want to play jump rope?" I smiled back at her and said, "Sure." As I began swirling the jump rope with Hannah, the gravity of her situation crushed me with its harshness.

At the time, Hannah was a young homeless girl living at the Union Rescue Mission, the largest and oldest homeless shelter in Los Angeles. Hannah was living there with her father, her younger sister, Savannah, just six years old, and her four-year-old brother, Nicholas. Reverend Andy Bales, the CEO of the Mission, was giving me a tour of the five-story, 225,000-square-foot building. Every weeknight between 5 p.m. and 6 p.m., the dozens of children that live there, Hannah among them, get to play in the gym.

The building is in the heart of Skid Row, an area in downtown Los Angeles that has one of the most highly concentrated areas of homelessness in the country; it is often called the only Third-World city in the nation. In a 50-block area, there are pimps and prostitutes, drug dealers and addicts, thieves, murderers, gang members, ex-convicts, rapists and pedophiles — and in this building, on the third floor, in a gymnasium inches away from this depraved city jungle, I met a little girl named Hannah.

When you think about Big Game networking, think about Hannah. She didn't think about what she wanted. She knew what she wanted and just asked for it. She didn't hesitate; she just walked up to me and asked a question. And through it all, as she was jumping up and down with a beaming smile on her face, she was having the best time of her life. Hannah unknowingly reminded me of the three most important skills in approaching Big Gamers — be bold, ask for what you want and have fun in the process.

If you can be like Hannah, then you will eventually develop the relationships you want, find the community of Big Gamers you desire and turn your most vivid dreams into your most memorable realities.

Aim high. When you serve others, it *is* worth it.

Acknowledgements

Whenever you watch a movie, you often only remember the riveting actors and actresses that breathe life into the film. And yet, it is also the team behind the scenes that contributes to the magic of what you see. A book is similar to a movie in that sense.

Although you have read my thoughts on paper, I want to thank my team behind the scenes that has helped me piece together a series of words, phrases and paragraphs into chapters, sections and a complete book.

First, I want to thank my mentor and friend Fred Joyal who inspired me with the term "Big Game," and Blake Nichols and Tyler Wagner who gave me the extra push I needed to start and finish this book. A special thanks to my brothers at METal International, a community of inspiring entrepreneurs and thought leaders: Ken Rutkowski, Mark Hattendorf, Larry Mondragon, Nolan Bushnell, Stephen Meade, Gregory Markel, Ken Kragen, Gene Lim, Christian Gray, Mike Reid, Mike Navarre, Edwin Benton, Yuri Moreira, Chris Biedryzski, Patrick Netter, Mark Goulston, Pascal Guyon, Mike Navarre, Joe Mulford, John Pastore, Vish Iyer, Ron Lin, Ali Binazir, Bart Baggett, Safa Sadeghpour, Mike Brooks, Lonnie Langdon, Adam Torres, and Ben Vanden Wymelenberg.

Thank you to my editors Megan Kimble, David Lott and Dina Del Valle, and to Keith Ferrazzi for your gracious foreword, as well as the numerous people who gave me invaluable feedback and help, including Barbara Brekke, Noel Croiger, Naheed Radfar, Hillary Gadsby, Justine Sophia, Maral Molleay, Ariel Yarrish, Dr. Marco Curreli, Mona Beaulieu, Angy Chin, Stella Song, Dennis Kneale, Michelle King Robson, Tim Chang, Antonio Spears, David Christopher Lee, Christine Van Loo, Michael Dee, Ravi Ananth, Craig Hasenbank, Kevin Lee, Jon Iadonisi, Kip Stringfellow, and Lynn Marks.

Thank you to Darin Leach and Thaddeus Vincent Krysius for creating my inspiring cover design and to Cindy Tyler, Lindsey Heath and Ashley Hemmen at Vervante for my book design and layout.

Lastly, I want to thank my family and friends, especially my mother, for instilling in me the iron discipline I apply to any project I create — including this book.

Appendix

Thank you for reading my book. If you enjoyed it, please write a review on Amazon.

If you have a Big Game networking success story, please share it with our community so you can inspire others at: www.facebook.com/biggamecommunity.

If you want to learn more about my services and products or receive my free newsletter filled with inspiring ways to meet Big Gamers, please sign up on my website: www.christopherkai.com

I always enjoy hearing from my readers. Please email me at: chris@christopherkai.com.

MY FAVORITE BOOKS BY OR ABOUT BIG GAMERS

Titan: The Life of John D. Rockefeller, Sr. by Ron Chernow

Steve Jobs by Walter Isaacson

Albert Einstein by Walter Isaacson

Principles by Ray Dalio

Autobiography: The Story of My Experiments with Truth by Mahatma Gandhi

The Autobiography of Dr. Martin Luther King, Jr. edited by Clayborne Carson

Bruce Lee: The Man Only I Knew by Linda Lee

The 7 Habits of Highly Effective People by Stephen R. Covey

I Am Malala: The Girl Who Stood Up for Education and was Shot by the Taliban by Malala Yousafzai

MY FAVORITE WEBSITES BY OR ABOUT BIG GAMERS

Wealth X
www.wealthx.com

Billionaires
www.billionaires.com

Luxury Institute
www.luxuryinstitute.com

Destination Luxury
www.destinationluxury.com

CEO
www.ceo.com

Bill Gates
www.gatesnotes.com

Sheryl Sandberg
www.leanin.org

Richard Branson
www.virgin.com/richard-branson

Mark Cuban
www.blogmaverick.com

Reid Hoffman
www.reidhoffman.org

Look to the Stars
www.looktothestars.org

BIG GAME COMMUNITY WEBSITES

World Economic Forum
www.weforum.org/communities

TED Conferences
www.ted.com/about/programs-initiatives

Milken Institute
www.milkeninstitute.org/events

Clinton Foundation
www.clintonfoundation.org

Entrepreneurs' Organization
www.eonetwork.org

Young Presidents' Organization
www.ypo.org

Notes

Introduction

1 http://abcnews.go.com/GMA/video?id=6106393

2 http://www.bls.gov/news.release/pdf/tenure.pdf

Chapter 2: Profile of a Big Gamer

3 http://www.sfgate.com/bayarea/article/A-DAY-IN-THE-LIFE-OF-Melanie-Craft-2804727.php

4 http://www.huffingtonpost.com/william-d-chalmers/the-great-american-passpo_b_1920287.html

Chapter 4: Know Your Why

5 http://www.bwater.com/Uploads/FileManager/Principles/Bridgewater-Associates-Ray-Dalio-Principles.pdf

Chapter 5: Give Them a Reason

6 http://blog.guykawasaki.com/2005/12/the_102030_rule.html

7 https://www.sequoiacap.com/grove/posts/yal6/elements-of-enduring-companies

8 https://www.americanexpress.com/us/small-business/openforum/articles/why-richard-branson-gave-400000-to-an-18-year-old

Chapter 7: Meet 'Those' People

9 http://business.financialpost.com/2014/09/19/alibaba-founder-jack-ma-from-school-teacher-to-chinas-richest-man

Chapter 11: Your Safari of Success

10 http://sv.thegmic.com/GMIC-Recap.pdf

11 http://techweek.com/who-attends

Chapter 23: Community First

12 http://www.entrepreneur.com/article/224168

Made in the USA
Columbia, SC
16 May 2022

60440070R00062